T0086718

CENOTAPH

2016 finalist
MILLER WILLIAMS
poetry prize

CENOTAPH

POEMS BY
BROCK JONES

The University of Arkansas Press
Fayetteville
2016

Copyright © 2016 by The University of Arkansas Press
All rights reserved
Manufactured in the United States of America

ISBN: 978-1-55728-172-2
e-ISBN: 978-1-61075-586-3
20   19   18   17   16   5   4   3   2   1

Designed by Liz Lester

⊗ The paper used in this publication meets the minimum
requirements of the American National Standard for Permanence
of Paper for Printed Library Materials Z39.48-1984.

Library of Congress Control Number: 2015952240

for Reisom Markose

SERIES EDITOR'S PREFACE

When the University of Arkansas Press asked if I would act as editor for the coming year's annual poetry prize named in honor of Miller Williams, the press's cofounder, long-time director, and progenitor of its poetry program, I was quick to accept. Since 1988 when he published my first full-length book, *The Apple That Astonished Paris,* I have felt indebted to Miller, who died in January 2015 at the age of eighty-four.

When he first spotted my poetry, I was forty-six years old with two chapbooks only. Not a pretty sight.

I have him to thank for first carrying me across that critical line dividing *no book* from *book*, thus turning me, at last, into a "published poet." I was especially eager to take on this task because it is a publication prize that may bring to light other first books. In fact, from the beginning of his time at the press, it was Miller's practice to publish one poet's first book every year. Then in 1990 this commitment was formalized when Miller awarded the first Arkansas Poetry Prize. Fittingly, it was renamed the Miller Williams Poetry Prize after his retirement and has grown to welcome work from both published and unpublished writers alike.

Miller Williams was more than my first editor. Over the years, he and I became friends, but even more importantly, before my involvement with the press, he served as a kind of literary father to me as his own straightforward, sometimes folksy, sometimes witty, and always trenchant poems became to me models of how poems could sound and how they could go. He was one of the poets who showed me that humor could be a legitimate mode in poetry—that a poem could be humorous without being silly or merely comical. He also showed me that a plain-spoken poem did not have to be imaginatively plain. Younger poets today could learn much from his example, as I did.

Given his extensive and distinguished career, it's surprising that Miller hasn't enjoyed a more prominent position on the American literary map. As his daughter became well known as a singer and recording artist, Miller became known to many as the father of Lucinda Williams. Miller and Lucinda even appeared on stage together several times performing a father-daughter act of song and poetry. And Miller enjoyed a bright, shining moment when Bill Clinton chose him to be the inaugural poet at his second inauguration in 1997. The poem he wrote for that day, "Of History and Hope," is a meditation on how "we have memorized America." In turning to the children of our country he broadens a nursery rhyme question by asking "How does our garden grow?" Occasional poems, especially for occasions of such importance, are notoriously difficult—some would say impossible—to write with success. But Miller rose to this lofty occasion and produced a winner. His confident reading of the poem before the nation added cultural and emotional weight to the morning's ceremony.

Apart from such public recognitions, most would agree that Miller's fuller legacy lies in his teaching and publishing career, which covered four decades. In that time, he published over a dozen books of his own poetry and literary theory. His accomplishments as a writing poet and working editor are what will speak for Miller in the years to come. The qualities of his poems make them immediately likeable and pleasurable. They sound as if they were spoken, not just written, and they show a courteous, engaging awareness of the presence of a reader. Miller knew that the idea behind a good poem is to make the reader feel something, rather than to merely display the poet's emotional state, which usually boils down to some form of misery. Miller also possessed the authority of experience to produce poems that were just plain wise.

With these attributes in mind, I began the judging of this year's prize. On the lookout for poems that Miller would approve of, that is, poems that seemed to be consciously or unconsciously in the Miller Williams School, I read and read. But in reading these scores of manuscripts, I realized that applying such narrow criteria would be selling Miller short. His tastes in poetry were clearly broader than the stylistic territory of his own verse; he published poets as different from one another as John Ciardi and Jimmy Carter. I readjusted and began to look for poems I thought Miller would delight in reading, instead of echoes of his own poems. This took some second-guessing, but I'm confident that Miller would enthusiastically approve of this year's selections.

Broadening the field of judgment brought happy results. The work of four very different poets, who have readability, freshness of language, and seriousness of intent in common, stood out among the stack of submissions.

Andrew Gent's [explicit lyrics] is a fascinating collection of poems that slip through their own cracks and seem to vanish before the reader's eyes. Influences are a matter of guesswork, but I'd say he has learned some of his admirable tricks from Yannis Ritsos and some of the New York School. Surprises lurk on almost every page. See You Soon, the casual title of Laura McKee's book, contains poems of powerful feeling that seem composed in the kind of tranquility of recollection, which Wordsworth recommended. Living in a country that appears to be continually involved in war on many fronts, readers will find in Brock Jones's *Cenotaph* a new way of thinking and feeling about the realities of combat. It is difficult to write war poetry because the subject is pre-loaded with emotional weight, but Jones more than manages to render precisely the mess of war with tenderness and insight. Joe Wilkins's poems are located in the tradition of the sacred, but holiness here is found in common experience. *When We Were Birds*, as the title indicates, is full of imaginative novelty as well as reminders that miraculous secrets are hidden in the fabric of everyday life.

In short we have here a gathering of young poets whose work, I think, would have fully engaged and gladdened Miller Williams. Because I have sat with him there, I can picture Miller in his study turning the pages, maybe stopping to make a pencil note in a margin. Miller's wider hope, of course, was that the poems published in this series would find a broad readership, ready to be delighted and inspired. I join my old friend and editor in that wish.

—*Billy Collins*

ACKNOWLEDGMENTS

A heartfelt thanks to the following journals in which many of these poems first appeared, often in different forms and with different titles: *Iowa Review, Lunch Ticket, Metaphor, Mobius: The Journal of Social Change, Mud Season Review, Naugatuck River Review, Ninth Letter, Raleigh Review,* and *Sugar House Review.*

This book would not have been possible without the help and support of so many others, and I wish to thank my family and friends who have supported me in every imaginable way. I hope you know who you are. Special thanks to Ryan Ikeda for being, most importantly, my friend and fellow wa(o)nderer. So many of these poems have benefited from your careful and enthusiastic reading.

Also, to Karin Anderson, Rob Carney, Katharine Coles, Andy Fitch, Laura Hamblin, Scott Hatch, Harvey Hix, Frieda Knobloch, Beth Loffreda, Kate Northrop, Jackie Osherow, Danielle Pafunda, and David Romtvedt, thank you for your kindness, support, and encouragement. I also want to thank the University of Wyoming Philosophy Department for seeing fit to award me with a James Orr Willits Ethics Award grant for travel and research that positively affected the writing of this book.

And finally, my deepest gratitude goes to AmyJo and Samantha, whose encouragement and love have never ceased to astound me. Without you, there would be no sunlight.

CONTENTS

PART TWO

And in the end, of course, a true war story
is never about war. It's about sunlight.

—Tim O'Brien's *The Things They Carried*

PART ONE

Facts

Call this irrefutable:
he was gone in minutes,

blood a hole in asphalt
deep enough to swallow sky.

But fact is boxes awaiting checkmarks
on a Casualty Feeder Card,

hollow water bottles
tumbling in rotorwash,

medic frantically
twisting a tourniquet

he knows has failed
but won't give up on.

Such are the details
we can't change: a heart

gasping for blood sputters
finally into emptiness.

But since this is our story
let's say he never realized he was dying

and slipped quietly off
the lip of his own life.

Say we had time and breath
enough for *Goodbye.*

Adios.
See you later. Be well.

Movie Night: Baghdad, April 2005

K-Mart announces he's putting a movie on and we pull camp chairs and cots to the center of the tent, around the TV, and Rich asks what we're watching and K-Mart says *Team America: World Police* which has to be hilarious, he says, since it was made by the same guys who make *South Park* and all the actors are puppets, which convinces us to give it a chance and he slips it in the player, and turns out most of us laugh pretty good here and there but none as hard as Markose, especially when the drunk marionette can't quit puking outside the bar, he can't stop laughing and keeps saying *Look at that shit!* and replays the scene at least three times, laughing harder and harder, and his laughing makes the rest of us laugh and by the third time we're all wiping tears from our eyes, and then a few of the guys say let the movie play on and he does, and when the movie's over, Markose, who will fight with his wife when this tour is over, get drunk and take a fistful of meds and never wake up, rewinds the DVD, his smile glowing in the light of the TV. *Man, we* gotta *see that again.*

Watercolor

I read an article about this artist who's been collecting those tiny photos of dead soldiers, the ones they put in the papers every week since '02. He says he can see the dead kid's *hope array*, he calls it, when he stares long enough at one of those photos, and then he paints it on a piece of that stiff paper and writes the name of the dead soldier at the bottom of the painting so he doesn't lose track of whose it is. He's got something like four hundred of these finished paintings stacked and hung in his apartment. Says he'd like to finish the project but can't seem to get the paintings done as fast as he used to since now, when he looks at a photo, all he can see is the face.

Field of View

What I remember—
the recoil, his fall
out of the scope's circle
into the burst hollow of his chest—

I will never forget.
As he emerged from the alley,
AK-47 concealed against his leg,
looking toward but not seeing us
on the roof, my bullet
already piercing his chest, perhaps

he remembered how his heart
leapt when his wife told him
of her dream in which their first son
was named by the prophet.

His hesitance to cross the street
face peering around the building corner
dustbloom at his fall
blood soaking his green shirt black

I remembered today as I looked
in the dictionary for a word I needed
but couldn't recall.

Alternate Ending

His hesitation
crosshairs settling
stiff recoil of the Barrett

I remembered today as I watched
Jimmy Fallon make music
with children's instruments.

Long Division

Shooters in Baghdad sometimes
waited in shut car trunks
to get a crack at U.S. soldiers,
one hole in a taillight
for the scope's line of sight
another for the bullet's path.
We were told to never stop moving.

Home now four months,
I know I should feel safe
but a university parking lot
offers so many places to hide

and if this tickle is a crosshair
settling at the center of my back
I'm gone before my cheek
bone shatters on asphalt.

So I rush the doors
knocking books out of a girl's hands
and don't even stop to help
because now I am
skimming the hallway wall
avoiding corners I can't see around
students leaning against windows

or walls or talking on phones
or reading walking laughing sitting.

Because what kills you is always concealed
so I turn into the first open doorway
on my side of the hall and find
a seat in the back.

This might be a story I tell for laughs
this weekend while baiting my catfish hook
with chicken liver down at the lake
except this is the second time in a week
I won't make it to anthropology
choosing instead to wait it out
in some other class.

Insomnia

The driver cannot sleep
until the child finishes her nightly

traverse of the sky, hopping from star to star,
pausing to dip her hand in the black river.

He wrote home of the man and woman
and the crushed car they'd escaped from

as his tank pancaked the trunk and back half
but he never mentioned

the wailing violence of their mourning,
their reaching with both hands toward the back seat,

the crushed glass of the rear window,
the still child's hand,

how he lies on his cot watching the girl
brush hair from her face and leap

empty space between steppingstones
on her way toward dawn.

Roads

The unit we replaced had named roads in our AO after porn stars, and we enjoyed those first mission briefings probably a little too much: *So we'll turn on Ariel*, the lieutenant would say, *then go down Jenna toward the house* . . . We came to know every curve and blind spot and pothole of Jasmine, Paige, Britney, and the rest. Months passed before the regimental commander caught wind of our beloved roads, had some staff officer rename them for colors and create new map overlays. Toward the end of our tour, some of us got to remembering Hemi and that medic from Delta who died when an IED took the back of the Bradley off clean, leaving both tracks intact and nothing where the crew compartment had been. *It was here*, Bennett said, tapping the map, *right here on Yellow*. Chief cursed and walked off lighting a Miami. He came back after a while with one of the old overlays, oriented it correctly over Bennett's map, and the argument was finally settled: *It may be Yellow to yous*, Chief said before sucking his cigarette, *but it will always be Olivia to me*.

Day after Equinox

I lie on my cot
dressing a hemorrhage

of stars, night still wounded
from yesterday's tracer rounds

and muzzle flash,
your letter across my chest:

How are you?
Has the weather changed there at all?
The rabbit brush along the tracks
in front of the house glows
like campfire in this light.

In the morning
I'll scrawl you a note

about the clarity of stars
over western Iraq

my wish for a change
of seasons, but will not name

the few facts I've learned
from this endless desert

or how I fear the nights
might seem colder now

the balance of day and night
has tilted, favoring darkness.

Pockets

Osh's cargo pockets split, spilling books he carried every patrol into the road like wrung-necked pigeons spinning dust circles, one wing propelling the spin with each downbeat, the other caught between limp body and road. We didn't take as a sign the coming apart of the books, their spines broken from use and heat, nor how they avoided retrieval when we halted the patrol to give Osh time to gather fistfuls of paper, nor that he boarded our flight home a few months after his pockets tore from the weight and friction of his superstition having, the night before, tossed the broken books, wing by wing, into the burn pit, nor the fact that both his pockets split open at precisely the same moment, the memory of which would set off a seizure of laughter among the small group of us huddled in the middle of a church three years later at his funeral.

Zero Gravity

Sitting in the gunner's strap
he dreamed the humvee
was a rocket lifting from earth
in a midnight storm of fire and smoke.

Once in orbit and free
of their body armor,
they bumped around the cab

roughhousing and happy
dodging rifles and helmets set adrift,
how long they'd been craving
weightlessness forgotten

until voices on the radio
propel him back to the turret,
the world cautiously resolving
back into familiar terms.

Machine gun.
Route recon patrol.
Kevlar and metal.
Gravity.

Where all mass-bearing words
eventually escape their orbits
and drift in the skull's
galaxy of vesicles and clefts.

Lifecycle

Inocula(ted)(tion) but not
immun(e)(ity),
power(less) again(st) this vector,
this agent memor(y)(ies)(ial)
in(fected)(jected).

Uncontroll(ed)(able) duplica(tion)(ting),
virions assemb(led)(ling),
viral proteins synthesiz(ing)(ed)(ation)
toward the memor(y's)(ies')(ial's)
trans(formation)(plantation)(action).

What anti(bodies)(dote)(thesis) have we
to fight com(pletion)(pression)(prehension)
of this violent
m(icro)(acro) human r(u)(a)pture,

myster(ious)(y) (mis)(un)read
this burst(ing) (ing) (ing), this
dis(order)(ruption)(aster)?

Waffle House, West Fillmore, April 2006

He says it's his turn to pay
so I wait by the door

on the far side of a mid-morning
crowd of diners waiting for seats.

Music trickles from ceiling speakers
barely heard over voices and coffee spoons.

A bald cook taps the grill with a spatula
and wipes his neck.

A couple holds
hands across a table.

Markose, who kills himself in four months,
passes bills over a counter

to a girl who says something
and points to the name on his uniform.

His response makes her laugh
as he gestures keep the change.

Handbook of Answers

Sunlight through the window
in skewed rectangles at my feet.
How's the war going?

Outside, clouds slide
toward a vanishing point
I believe in more than see.
What's it like over there?

You see any combat?
A crow flies across
the screen of the window.

Is it as bad as they say?
You kill anyone?

What's it like?

I.

like a window
like a clean window
like a rain-splattered window
like a cracked window
like a broken window
like a shattered window
like a window frame
like a window pane
like a window screen
like an open window
like a half-open window
like a closed window
like a window painted shut

II.

like the first minute of sunlight
like morning sunlight
like midday sunlight
like afternoon sunlight
like the last minute of sunlight
like waiting for sunlight
like wishing for sunlight
like hiding from sunlight
like escaping from sunlight
like praying for sunlight
like asking for sunlight
like looking for sunlight
like missing the sunlight
like hating the sunlight
like needing the sunlight
like hating the sunlight
like needing the sunlight
like hating sunlight
like needing sunlight

III.

like last decade
like last year
like last month
like last week
like day before yesterday
like yesterday
like an hour ago
like now
like in three hours
like tomorrow
like day after tomorrow
like next week
like next month
like next year
like next decade

IV.

like nothing
like everything
like something
like anything
like no everything
like no something
like no anything
like every nothing
like every something
like every anything
like some nothing
like some everything
like some anything
like any nothing
like any everything
like any something

V.

like a monument
like stone as monument
like tree as monument
like river as monument
like photo as monument
like memories as monuments
like songs as monuments
like diners as monuments
like streets as monuments
like cities as monuments
like Utah as monument
like Wyoming as monument
like Colorado as monument

VI.

like rabbit brush
like rabbit brush along back roads
like rabbit brush along train tracks
like rabbit brush along highways
like rabbit brush in August
like rabbit brush in September
like rabbit brush blooming in September
like rabbit brush in October
like rabbit brush in November

VII.

like a dream in color
like a dream in black and white
like a dream you remember
like a dream you want to remember
like a dream you almost remember
like a dream you can't remember
like a dream you don't remember
like a dream you don't want to remember
like a dream you want to forget
like a dream you never forget
like a dream you want to wake from
like a dream you know you're dreaming
like a dream you never want to wake from
like a dream you can't tell anyone
like a dream that can't be told
like a dream that can't be held
like a dream that can't be touched
like a dream that can't be said
like a dream that can't be dreamed

VIII.

like across
like after
like against
like around
like before
like behind
like below
like beneath
like beside
like between
like beyond
like in
like inside
like near
like on
like onto
like outside
like over
like through
like throughout
like to
like toward
like under
like underneath
like within
like without

IX.

like
like
like
like
like
like

Alternate Ending

His hesitation to cross
the street, the recoil
our celebration

I remembered today looking
at photos of my parents
on their wedding day.

Arkansas

We meet at the wall of 4,000 stars
and I almost speak but choose instead

to silently follow my grandpa,
dead eight years ago this summer,

to the Atlantic pavilion engraved
with foreign names he never forgot.

Bastogne.
Yeah, we was there.

St. Marie Eglise.
We was near there.

St. Lo.
A beautiful place before we got there.

Berlin.
War got good then.

I follow him around the plaza's center pool
until he stops, hand in pocket,

in front of ARKANSAS,
home state of his best war buddy, Chitty,

fellow machine gunner cut in half
in a sawmill accident a few years after the war.

The tourist crowd I came early to avoid
is filling the monument now.

Go on along feller, he says, *I'll catch up*.
I turn before ascending the stairs: He stands,

a hunched figure, in front of ARKANSAS.
Still, in front of ARKANSAS.

Playlist Autobiography 1976–2006

God Bless the U.S.A. (Lehi, Utah, 1981)
    Dad
    windows down in the Ford
    singing

We Built This City (Moscow, Idaho, 1985)
    Claire
    flip-digit clock radio
    waking from crush-dreams

Girl You Know It's True (Alpine, Utah, 1989)
    Jona
    blue-carpet basement
    playing Tip-In and talking girls

New Sensation (Alpine, Utah, 1990)
    Dad
    cussing Sal's
    black clothes

Like a Lighthouse (Alpine, Utah, 1991)
    Mom
    bran muffin batter
    into cupcake pans

Gimme Back My Bullets (Lehi, Utah, 1991)
    Levi
    nine-ball
    and frozen Twinkies

Rock You Like a Hurricane (Vernal, Utah, 1993)
    pre-game
    pump-up music

Free Fallin' (Wellington, Utah, 1994)
    Kalie
    Highway 6 headwind
    driving from Bullfrog to Price

Lady in Red (Salt Lake City, Utah, 1995)
    Michelle
    dancing slow
    state-capital prom

A Whiter Shade of Gray (Santa Fe, Argentina, 1996)
    ruptured appendix
    peritonitis haze

Jeremy (Tooele, Utah, 1998)
    Uncle Bruce

Hurt (Fort Carson, Colorado, 2003)
    K-Mart and Duree
    night shift
    gate guard

Wanted Dead or Alive (Fort Carson, Colorado, 2003)
    pre-deployment briefings:
    culture language religion

Adagio Sostenuto (Al Qaim, Iraq, 2003)
    Grandpa Jones
    imagining myself present
    at his graveside service

Come Away with Me (Al Asad Airbase, Iraq, 2003)
    army cot
    adrift in the Milky Way

Bodies (Fort Carson, Colorado, 2004)
    post-deployment slideshow:
    blasts shots rockets

When I Look to the Sky (Orem, Utah, 2004)
    AmyJo

Cannonball (Tal Afar, Iraq, 2005)
    rooftop boots off
    choppers overhead

Home (Sinjar, Iraq, 2005)

Holy Water (Lehi, Utah, 2006)
    AmyJo
    singing harmony
    in my pickup

Life Ain't Always Beautiful (Lehi, Utah, 2006)
    Markose
    crossing the Jordan
    on the old iron bridge

Invocation

Words vaulting
through a chapel,

petitions murmured into fists,
hymn or anthem notes

filling organ pipes,
sunlight's missive

whispered through stained glass,
rifle blasts bounding

down perfect granite lines.
The epics have already been written.

Pardon these thick lead cames
between panes of bright glass

all the crossouts and misspellings
of this handwritten note.

PART TWO

Hypothermia

Let us pool our heat,
avoiding for one more night

questions that will still be questions
tomorrow, holding what seeks escape

in the combined light
of our separate flickerings

like two candles burning
in the cold black window.

Four Obituaries

July 11

When one of his guys' AC units breaks
he refuses to run the one in his room

they love him for it.

But even *tactical patience*
conceals its own lifespan

      after so much lifting
dead boys, sealing body bags
     children in a crossfire
        cries of mothers.

No more singing Sesame Street
        while on patrol

August 9

He'd come home
from the second tour

slamming the door
of their new apartment.

March 19

He returns from Iraq on the 15th:

I feel invisible.
Transparent.

January 1

They make him wear a trash-bag poncho
corrective training for being *dirty*.

He heads to the shitter
only place to be alone.

There will be corrective action
discipline
a *Wall of Discipline*
chain of command

no longer.

July 11

His driver said he turned
his head but not enough not in time,

was in the seat next to him when
he kicked open the humvee door,

witnessed the perfect fit
of the M4 muzzle in the hollow
of the lower jaw.

Swears he saw him slightly turn
an instant before the rifle blast
like he'd remembered something
too late

August 9

Police find him
facedown on the carpet:

Wellbutrin and whiskey
after a fight with his wife.

*Symptoms include nausea, vomiting,
delirium and seizures,
auditory and visual hallucinations.*

Bupropion overdose rarely results in death.

March 19

Hanging in his barracks room,
wounds from yesterday's
attempt bandaged still
blood-stained carpet bloody still

and him swaying
slowly above it all
when CQ comes to check on him
sometime after 1

January 1

Bullet through the forehead,
black river coursing the creases
of his trash-bag poncho
pooling around his boots.

August 9

You died alone

but I imagine us all there—
Will, J.R., Cooper,
Hopewell, Petey, Rich, Weaver—
through the seizures and
stomach cramps

July 11

*Close your eyes and think of me
and Jeremy and James,* she'd said.

That final phone call home
and the turning
of the head
like a wish

poorly heard in the wind.

helping you off the floor
into the shower

and closing the door
behind you when you left
to find her.

March 19

January 1

*I really don't know what to say
in a note like this.
I just don't feel good
about what I've accomplished
in my life. I feel like a failure.*

*And there's no hope of improving.
Been a couple places in the army
and it's all been pretty much the same.*

July 11

Every body bag you zipped
ripped bigger the hole.

Every death you *should* have
prevented
every loss you *should* have
prevented
every boy you *should* have
saved:

narrowing increments
between that muzzle and your
chin.

August 9

March 19

January 1

Investigators:

*death may have been
prevented.*

July 11

Sunny Day
Sweepin' the clouds away
On my way to where the air is sweet!

You couldn't prevent any-
body's suffering.

Not so simple
as turning your head
before the blast,
dodging the bullet

staying in the humvee. | August 9

March 19 | January 1

July 11 | August 9

March 19 | January 1

Alternate Ending

His green shirt
the recoil
his fall
our exultation

I remembered today standing
in the shower rinsing
soap from my face.

Eleven Mile

for J.R.

You hook another rainbow and I forget
the drift of my tattered fly.

Yet to land a fish, I have no way out
of buying dinner since that's the usual deal

and there's no way to catch you
with three fish before dark.

But this memory does not want to be
about fishing or whether real fishermen

use spinners or flies, who caught the most fish,
where to eat dinner on our way back to post,

our return from Iraq to ticker-tape,
drinks on the house and eventual emptiness.

It wants to be about sunlight
reflecting off our favorite river

today same as it did then, before falling
behind those Colorado mountains.

Maybe it is about fishing after all.
It can be about fishing.

The Less We Know

Like when some poor grunt disappears off the face of the earth in an explosion and you can't help think that maybe somehow he's hitchhiked down to the Gulf. Flip-flops and shorts, surf to his knees, watching the horizon. A scout in Bravo lost one of his buddies that way. One minute he's there and the next . . . dust. They searched three days, found a helmet and a foot in a boot and some other pieces. Wasn't more than a few weeks after that the scout went to take a piss and heard his old pal's muffled voice calling to him from deep down in one of the PVC pipes sticking out of the ground where everyone in camp went to relieve themselves. And so when he recognized his buddy's voice coming out of that three-inch pipe, he wouldn't let anyone else near the place and even locked and loaded his M4, that's how serious he was. His first sergeant and a few other NCOs finally had to get involved and when they tackled him he hugged so tightly to that one piss tube he pulled it out of the ground as they dragged him off.

Translation

The fist-sized exit wound,
a wide mouth filled with broken teeth,
bleeds surprisingly little
on the inside of the man's thigh.
Had the bullet split the artery
like it did bone
he would already be dead.

Doc Guerrero fingers gauze
into the wound and the man screams,
grabs my arm and doesn't let go
even after Doc finishes splinting the leg.

An older Iraqi man sitting
ziptied and blindfolded against a humvee tire
lifts his head when the screaming stops.

The wounded man asks for a translator
Mutergem? Mutergem?
one of the few Arabic words I know,
and I shake my head.
"We don't have one. *La mutergem.*"
With crude hand signals I try
to make him understand words
like helicopter and hospital
but he shakes his head
and asks again softly. *Mutergem?*

When the medevac helicopter
swings around to land
the man grabs my hand with both of his
and I feel self-conscious
holding hands with him crying.

I try to free myself from his grip
as he's talking directly at me in Arabic
now and I yell over the noise of the bird
"You gotta let go, man. You'll be fine!"
but he won't let go.

When we slide him,
strapped tightly to the stretcher,
into the helicopter
I have to free myself from him
finger by finger so I can back off
enough for the chopper to lift
into the cloudless sky.

Through the dustoff
I see him reaching toward me
crying still, speaking words
I cannot hear.

Immunity

When he kneels
armed with a rectangle of cardboard

torn off a box of MREs
to scoop the mound of red spume

B left us to clean up
after he shot himself in the head,

he wonders if immunity
to blood is acquired or innate.

Even as he makes as if he might puke,
mouth pressed against his arm

wishing there was more to feel
than the shock of cooled blood

through latex gloves.
Even as he fights an impulse to fake

another dry-heave and shakes
clotted blood from his cardboard

into a garbage bag.
Even as he reaches down for more.

Survivor

The leg grew back
skin first, like an empty
sock, then bone
into the proper form
of a foot.

Visitors came
from across the state
once the facts were leaked.

But re-growing a leg
is pain almost impossible
to bear he wanted to tell them

and his new toes throb
nonstop since the day
he woke in the hospital

a Lazarus in a new world
filled with all the old wonders
except resurrection
of friends killed
in the blast
that took his leg.

Three Sisters

These tiny date palms
whisper to each other

hands over mouths
to grab the tails of errant vowels

Eyes a hue
there is no name for

Tangled-hair coronas
of sunlight

Toes like roots hold them
fast in memory

but even rock turns to sand
when exposed to this endless wind.

Rock, Paper, Scissors

Loser had to drag sloshing half-barrels
from under the wooden latrines

add diesel and stir with blackened
picket, then toss flaming wands

of *Stars and Stripes* into each.
By the time the barrels needed a second stir

we'd be throwing hard as we could,
raggedy mitts popping like distant rifles.

We even considered volunteering for this detail,
the obvious downside to the job ignored,

once the ball gloves and baseball
arrived in a package from home.

We'd give each other our best stuff
until the fifth or sixth stir

then stand around the fading fires
kneading tired arms, welcoming the ache.

Incoming, 3 a.m.

Finishing up what had become his nightly after-midnight piss, a ball of light unzipped the darkness above him, lighting the desert all the way to Syria. He fell next to a humvee tire and folded in on himself like a fist, saw the guys finding him dead come morning with his junk half out his pants. But the incoming rocket was actually a shooting star, brightest he'd ever seen, and he stood up and laughed. Was still chuckling as he made his way back up to the roof where he and a few others slept in the open air, shaking his head and quietly laughing as he pulled off boots stiff with the day's sweat, thinking it a shame to waste a laugh like that, wishing someone else had been awake to see him dive for cover in that eruption of light.

Alternate Ending

I remembered today while spinning
my little girl in a tire swing at the park.

His fall.
My exultation.

Wreckage

The night of the funeral, her sobs
crumble the foundation, bringing
the house to rubble around her
as she sits under a creased-flag blanket,
back against the front door.

As a sinkhole yawns to swallow
the house, she takes to the air,
flag-cape cracking behind her.

By the time she sees the lights of Denver
the pain in the back of her legs from the flag-whipping
reminds her she doesn't know how to fly

and she sinks through wet clouds,
failed flag-parachute tangled
around her plunging figure.

It takes all night to gather and fit
the immense span of her wreckage
into a flag-satchel for the long walk home.

Alternate Ending

I remembered today while lying
next to Amy
holding hands in bed.

Alternate Ending

I remembered today as I rode
the train downtown.

Along the Road to Bi'aj

Even if science explains
how randomly a body

disintegrates in a blast
this would still not make sense:

penis
human face
a hand, two feet
pile of something bloody
car pieces
crater.

Next week or years from now
when he thinks of this day

he will lose his appetite
in the DFAC with the guys,

or at dinner with his wife,
with Paul at the game,

but right now there's nothing
but to laugh:

a fleshy churro rolled in sand,
bearded face skin a cheap horror-flick gag,

armless hand cupped
holding dense morning sunlight.

He chooses his path slowly
through this human debris field

taking pictures and laughing
as only the living can.

Memorial from a Park Bench

Here's an opened book.
Stranger you greet like a friend
with reciprocated kiss.
Here, touch is required.

Visitors descend to meet
names arranged in order.
A word loses its ability to conjure
trapped inside a black mirror.

The names could be lines
of poems or a grocery list.
They could be just lines
but even before
you're close enough to read
you know they are names
because everyone knows
the names.

Here is name
stacked on names stacked
on panels of more.
Here are names and black stone
and your only reflection.

Waffle House, Jimmy Carter Blvd., Jan. 2014

What did I believe I would find
at this diner, empty of all but light?

Knowing none of the guys would be here,
that he wouldn't be here

and I'd stare into empty booths for an hour,
filling them with ghosts and wishes

I carry with me
from Utah, Colorado, Iraq?

Because this is where we'd meet
if he were alive, where he'd expect me

to find him with slap hug, wide smile,
then silence while we ate.

Because hope is a pull string
in the dark we find only

when it brushes our face
in the wild-arm search for bare light.

Gift of Tongues

He wrote a letter to his girlfriend describing the deaths of the Iraqi men like something he'd seen once in a movie, then tossed the sealed envelope into the burn pit and never spoke of it until a month after coming back to Carson from block leave, as the staff duty NCO half carried him to his room. *Wasn't the smell of burning men what caused me to piss myself, you know that? But how could I understand every word of the prayer they choked on as they fell?*

Rogue Memories

Curator of the National Archive of Collective Memory and War Memorabilia called with concerns about some of my facts, dates and names and other details his office had been trying to *independently verify* for some time now. A number of incongruities in my stories have caused uncertainty *in certain circles* as to whether or not I was really even in Iraq at all, he said. I got a little defensive and paused to swallow before asking him where it was he thought all these memories came from. But the curator assured me it wasn't worth getting *too worked up about*, they were *just following protocol after all*. Perhaps the memories were stories I'd told myself so long now that they may as well be mine, he said, stories based on bits of movies and books I'd seen or read, or heard others tell over the years. *We simply can't be too careful, you understand, about the damage to the integrity of the archive even one rogue memory could cause. I'm sure you know this, Mr. Jones—though it never hurts to be reminded—that when all else has failed, only* truth *will set you free.*

Postlude

And the final clench-
ing of teeth

whine of the body-
bag zipper

*Adios: Later man: Good -
bye: See you   on the flip side.*